LIBRARY

Gift of the
Amnesty International Club
1991

THE UNIVERSAL DECLARATION OF HUMAN RIGHTS

AN ADAPTATION FOR CHILDREN
BY RUTH ROCHA AND OTAVIO ROTH

UNITED NATIONS PUBLICATIONS
Copyright © United Nations 1989
All rights reserved
Manufactured in Brazil by Salamandra Editorial

THE UNIVERSAL DECLARATION OF HUMAN RIGHTS.

AN ADAPTATION FOR CHILDREN BY RUTH ROCHA AND OTAVIO ROTH

ONE DAY,
A LARGE NUMBER OF PEOPLE
         GATHERED TOGETHER.

THEY CAME FROM DIFFERENT PLACES
AND THEY WERE QUITE DIFFERENT
FROM ONE ANOTHER.

SOME WERE MEN AND SOME WERE
WOMEN.
THEIR SKIN,
  THEIR HAIR AND THEIR EYES
        WERE DIFFERENT COLOURS.
THEIR BODIES AND FACES WERE
           DIFFERENT SHAPES.

THEY CAME FROM RICH COUNTRIES AND
POOR COUNTRIES, FROM HOT PLACES
AND COLD PLACES.

SOME CAME FROM KINGDOMS
        AND SOME CAME FROM REPUBLICS.
THEY SPOKE MANY DIFFERENT LANGUAGES.
THEY WORSHIPPED DIFFERENT GODS.

SOME OF THE COUNTRIES THEY REPRESENTED
HAD JUST COME OUT OF A TERRIBLE WAR
THAT HAD LEFT MANY CITIES
DESTROYED
AND AN ENORMOUS NUMBER OF PEOPLE
KILLED.
MANY PEOPLE HAD LOST THEIR HOMES
AND THEIR FAMILIES.

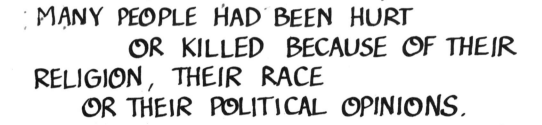

MANY PEOPLE HAD BEEN HURT
OR KILLED BECAUSE OF THEIR
RELIGION, THEIR RACE
OR THEIR POLITICAL OPINIONS.

WHAT BROUGHT THOSE PEOPLE TOGETHER
WAS THE WISH THAT
THERE SHOULD BE NO MORE WAR,
THAT NOBODY SHOULD EVER
BE HURT AGAIN AND THAT
PEOPLE WHO HADN'T DONE
OTHER PEOPLE ANY HARM
SHOULD NEVER BE PUNISHED AGAIN.

SO, ALL TOGETHER,
THEY WROTE A DOCUMENT.
IN THIS DOCUMENT THEY TRIED
  TO MAKE A LIST
OF THE RIGHTS THAT
    EVERY HUMAN BEING HAS,
AND THAT EVERYONE ELSE
    SHOULD
RESPECT.

THIS DOCUMENT IS CALLED
    THE UNIVERSAL DECLARATION OF
            HUMAN RIGHTS ;
    AND THIS IS WHAT IT SAYS:

ALL PEOPLE ARE BORN FREE.
ALL PEOPLE ARE BORN EQUAL AND SO
PEOPLE CAN THINK FOR
THEMSELVES
AND UNDERSTAND WHAT
EVERYONE SHOULD ACT AS
BROTHERS AND
SISTERS.

HAVE EQUAL RIGHTS.

GOING ON AROUND THEM.

IT DOESN'T MATTER WHAT RACE YOU ARE.
IT DOESN'T MATTER WHETHER
YOU'RE A MAN OR A WOMAN.
IT DOESN'T MATTER WHAT LANGUAGE
YOU SPEAK,
WHAT YOUR RELIGION IS,
WHAT YOUR POLITICAL OPINIONS ARE,
WHAT COUNTRY YOU COME FROM OR
WHO YOUR FAMILY IS.
IT DOESN'T MATTER WHETHER YOU'RE
RICH OR POOR.
IT DOESN'T MATTER WHAT PART OF THE
WORLD YOU COME FROM;
WHETHER YOUR COUNTRY
IS A KINGDOM OR A REPUBLIC.
THESE RIGHTS AND FREEDOMS ARE MEANT
TO BE ENJOYED BY
EVERYONE.

EVERYONE HAS THE RIGHT
TO LIVE,
THE RIGHT TO BE FREE AND
THE RIGHT TO
PERSONAL SAFETY.
NO ONE
CAN BE SOMEONE
ELSE'S
SLAVE.

NO ONE
IS TO BE HURT
OR TO BE
PUNISHED IN CRUEL
OR
HUMILIATING WAYS.

THE LAW MUST B
THE LAW MUST
PEOPLE HAVE THE RIGHT TO B
SO THAT THEI

HE SAME FOR EVERYONE.
ROTECT EVERYONE.
ROTECTED BY THE COURTS,
IGHTS ARE RESPECTED.

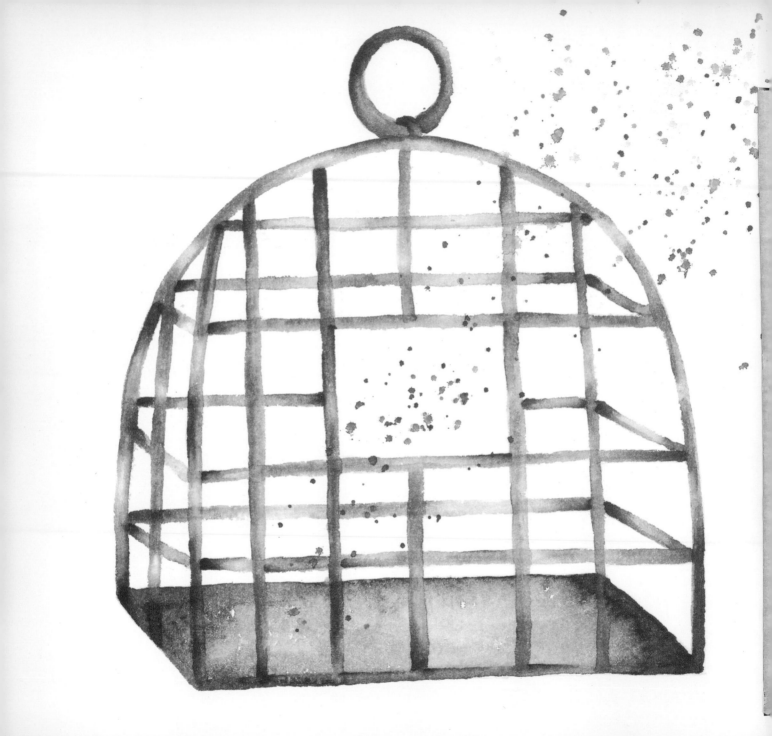

PEOPLE CANNOT BE ARRESTED,
    OR SENT AWAY FROM THEIR COUNTRY,
UNLESS IT'S FOR A VERY SERIOUS REASON.
EVERYONE HAS THE RIGHT
    TO A FAIR TRIAL.

NO ONE HAS THE RIGHT TO INTERFER
IN THEIR FAMILIES, IN THEIR HOME:

N OTHER PEOPLE'S PRIVATE LIVES,
OR IN THEIR CORRESPONDENCE.

PEOPLE HAVE THE RIGHT OF FREE MOVEMENT
WITHIN THEIR COUNTRY.
PEOPLE HAVE THE RIGHT TO LEAVE ANY COUNTRY,
EVEN THEIR OWN, AND THEN RETURN.

NO PERSON OR PEOPLE SHALL HAVE
    THEIR NATIONALITY TAKEN AWAY FROM THEM.
THIS MEANS EVERYONE HAS THE RIGHT
        TO BELONG
            TO A NATION.

AND THEY ALSO HAVE THE RIGHT TO CHANGE
THEIR NATIONALITY, IF THEY WANT TO.

ALL MEN AND WOMEN HAVE THE RIGHT
TO GET MARRIED AND START A FAMILY,
ONCE THEY'VE REACHED A CERTAIN AGE.
IT DOESN'T MATTER WHAT RACE,
NATIONALITY OR RELIGION THEY ARE.
A MAN AND A WOMAN CAN ONLY GET MARRIED
IF THEY BOTH WANT TO.

EVERYONE HAS THE RIGHT
TO OWN PROPERTY.
ANYTHING THAT BELONGS TO A PERSON
CAN'T BE TAKEN AWAY
FROM HIM OR HER
UNLESS THERE'S A FAIR REASON.

EVERYONE HAS THE RIGHT TO
PEOPLE HAVE THE RIGHT TO HOLD OPINIONS AND
AND THEY HAVE THE RIGHT TO PRACTICE

HINK THE WAY THEY LIKE.
D TELL OTHER PEOPLE WHAT THEIR OPINIONS ARE.
HEIR RELIGION IN PRIVATE OR IN PUBLIC.

ALL PEOPLE HAVE THE RIGHT TO MEET
TOGETHER AND TO FORM ASSOCIATIONS.
BUT NO ONE CAN BE FORCED TO JOIN AN
ASSOCIATION IF HE OR SHE DOESN'T WANT TO.

A GOVERNMENT'S
AUTHORITY COMES FROM THE WILL
OF THE PEOPLE.
PEOPLE MUST SHOW WHAT THEY WANT THEIR
GOVERNMENT TO DO BY VOTING.
EVERYONE HAS THE RIGHT TO VOTE.

EVERYONE HAS THE RIGHT TO WORK.
AND PEOPLE HAVE THE RIGHT TO CHOOSE
THE KIND OF JOB THEY WANT TO DO.
EVERYONE HAS THE RIGHT TO
GOOD WORKING CONDITIONS.
EVERYONE HAS THE RIGHT TO EQUAL PAY
FOR EQUAL WORK.
PEOPLE SHOULD EARN ENOUGH TO KEEP
THEMSELVES AND THEIR FAMILIES HEALTHY,
TO GIVE THEM ENOUGH FOOD TO EAT
AND ENOUGH CLOTHES TO WEAR,
SOMEWHERE TO LIVE, AND MEDICAL
ATTENTION WHEN THEY'RE ILL.

EVERYONE HAS THE RIGHT TO REST.
THEY SHOULD HAVE A LIMITED NUMBER
OF WORKING HOURS
AND SHOULD STILL BE PAID
WHILE THEY'RE ON
HOLIDAY.

ALL CHILDREN HAVE THE SAME RIGHTS,
WHETHER THEIR PARENTS ARE MARRIED
OR NOT.

EVERYONE HAS THE RIGHT
TO GO TO SCHOOL
AND SCHOOL MUST BE FREE.
EVERYONE SHOULD HAVE
THE RIGHT TO BE
TAUGHT A TRADE.
EDUCATION SHOULD
EMPHASISE
UNDERSTANDING,
COMPREHENSION,
TOLERANCE
AND FRIENDSHIP.

PEOPLE HAVE DUTIES
    TOWARDS THE PLACE
        WHERE THEY LIVE
AND TOWARDS OTHER PEOPLE WHO
        LIVE THERE WITH THEM.

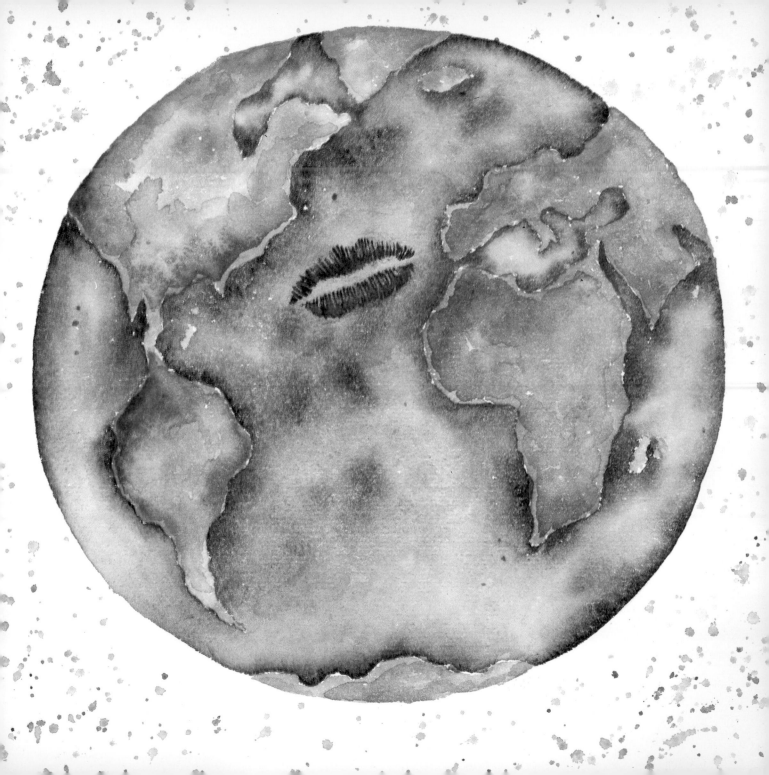

NOTHING THAT IS WRITTEN
   IN THIS DOCUMENT MAY BE USED
 TO JUSTIFY TAKING AWAY
   THE RIGHTS AND FREEDOMS
SET OUT IN THIS DECLARATION.

MANY YEARS AGO THIS DECLARATION
WAS APPROVED,
HOWEVER, NOT ALL COUNTRIES
RESPECT THIS DOCUMENT.
AND THIS IS WHY EVERYONE OUGHT TO
READ THIS DOCUMENT,
AND WHY IT SHOULD BE TAUGHT
IN SCHOOLS
ALL OVER THE WORLD.

This book was written by Ruth Rocha and illustrated by Otavio Roth to promote and disseminate the contents of the Universal Declaration of Human Rights among children all over the world. By adapting the original text into an easier language the authors hope to make these ideas better known, accepted and respected by everyone.

Ruth Rocha was born in São Paulo, Brazil. A sociologist, she worked for many years in education before becoming a successful writer. She is the author of more than 80 titles published in Brazil, Argentina, Spain and England. Since 1976 her books have sold over 3 million copies, which has made Ruth Rocha one of the most popular and prestigious Brazilian writers.

Otavio Roth was born in São Paulo, Brazil. He has a degree in art and design and has lived and worked in London, Oslo, New York and San Francisco. His prints, drawings and paper installations have been widely exhibited in museums and galleries since 1972, in the United States, Japan, Brazil and various European countries. Roth's original linocut prints on the human rights theme belong to important collections all over the world, including the United Nations in New York, Vienna and Geneva.

Sales no. 89.I.19
ISBN 92-1-100423-3